Published by 4th Monkey
Windsor, UK

www.myofficetoday.co.uk
email: melgow@me.com

ISBN 978-0-9555921-1-9

British Library Cataloguing in Publication Data
A complete catalogue record for this book can be obtained from the British Library on request

Cover design by Loulita Gill
Original cover image by Melanie Gow
All images and text by Melanie Gow
Editing by John Pring and Sinead Fitzgibbon
Portrait photographs of Melanie Gow by Daria Marczak
Printed through SS Media Ltd, Hertfordshire

There is a feeling you can only get when the unknown meets with your open mind;
a closed door lets nothing in

PROLOGUE

I am an ordinary mother who left home one day to go for a walk with her two sons, aged 12 and 16, for 33 exceptional days, over the Pyrenees and across Spain for 800 kilometres to Santiago de Compostela.

I wanted to give my sons something they would remember all their lives. I also knew that it would be precious time that I could spend with them, before they left home.

I really hoped it would be a space in which my sons could choose what kind of men they wanted to be.

It turned out that it really was the best thing I could have done for them, and it was the very best thing I could have done with them. But the most surprising thing was that somewhere during that stroll across a country, I went through a profoundly transformative experience.

It was a walk that gently changed our lives.

It all started on an unassuming Tuesday night in February with a plate of sausage, mash, and peas, with gravy, in front of a film. There was the usual wrangling to get my boys off their computer games, and email alerts were going off demandingly while I juggled household chores. There was nothing about that evening that even hinted that it would turn out to be the start of something extraordinary.

That night we put on *The Way*, a film by Martin Sheen that is essentially about a handful of middle-aged people walking and talking.

It is a fictional account of a man who walks a pilgrim route called The Camino after his son dies in the attempt, and the stories of those he meets on the journey. As the end credits rolled both boys stood up and simply said that they wanted to walk it.

Have you ever really wanted to do something, for which you have no rational reason or explanation, except you just wanted to do it? This was it for us, and we had to do it together.

5

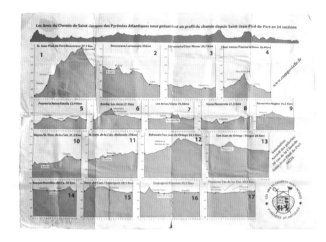

This medieval pilgrimage known as The Camino, which means "the path" in Spanish, has been walked in much the same way for centuries.

The path is even older than that. It follows the Milky Way and pagans used it to cross northern Spain in a ritual of death and rebirth. They walked to La Costa de Morte (the Coast of Death) on the Pacific Ocean, finishing at Fisterra, which means "the end of the world". They then burnt their clothes and made offerings and rites in honour of the sun, before watching it fall into the infinite sea.

Pilgrimages to Jerusalem, in the Holy Land, began in the fourth century, during the rule of Constantine, the first Roman emperor to convert to Christianity. They were popular until the advent of the Crusades made Jerusalem too dangerous for pilgrims, and Rome and Santiago were declared destinations to compensate.

It became necessary for pilgrimage sites to possess relics to ensure their importance in the Christian faith. The Apostle James is known to have spent a number of years preaching in the Iberian Peninsula, home to the city of Santiago, until he was beheaded when he returned to Jerusalem.

His remains are believed to have returned to Spain and held in Santiago de Compostela; by the 13th century The Camino, also known as The Way of St. James, became one of the most important Christian pilgrimages.

Wars between Spain and England, and the Reformation, followed by the Enlightenment, and topped off by a little Franco, meant pilgrimages went out of fashion for hundreds of years.

Until 1987, when Paulo Coelho wrote about his experience of walking The Camino in *The Pilgrimage*. Then a German comedian brought out a book, as did a Korean woman, then Martin Sheen made a film, and now my sons wanted to walk it with me…

With three people in a room wanting to do the same thing, it seemed easy to say yes.

After all, how hard could it be? It was just a long walk…

It was the hardest thing I have ever done, physically, mentally, and emotionally. It was also the very best thing I have ever done, for that same reason.

We were unprepared, underfunded, and unfit. However, I wanted to approach it as an extension of life. There are many times when we have to face a challenge and we need a little grit and a little trust in ourselves. We have to learn to take a chance, step outside our comfort zone, and realise the worst thing that can happen is that we learn a valuable life lesson.

In the extreme, there are those who are made homeless by conflict or disaster so have to walk for many days to safety, with no warning or training, and I felt we could manage this.

We deliberately didn't take a guidebook; I reasoned that we aren't given a guidebook for the journey through life so why should this journey be any different? On a practical level, guidebooks are heavy and take up space in your baggage. Without a guidebook to depend on, we knew we would have

to interact with people, to ask for directions, advice and help, and that would be all the better for making friends. We would also have to make an effort to find out about interesting places ourselves; some of our best memories have come from putting a guidebook down and allowing things to cross our path naturally. Without a guidebook there is the possibility of coming to know the joy of discovery.

If you think that is cavalier, it is wise to remember that a guidebook can tell you where a water fountain is, but it cannot tell you if the water is contaminated.

We left home with little more than a trust in our own resources, the desire to do it, and the willingness to accept the experience. Perhaps most importantly, we believe life is a brief shot at something incredible.

After 19 hours by underground, coach, taxi, train, and bus we arrived at St Jean Pied de Port, nestled in the shadow of the Pyrenees Mountains on the French side. You can think of the town as a point of convergence for all the routes from the east. We had

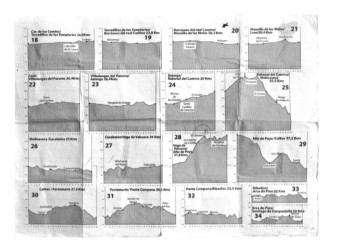

our Credentials stamped; these are equivalent to pilgrim passports, in the past they ensured you safe passage. Now you get them stamped all along the route to show you have walked it. We were handed a map: two sides of an A4 photocopied piece of paper. This was an outline of the days ahead, and it told you everything you really needed to know. It showed height above sea level up the side and kilometres along the bottom, roughly evenly divided into days.

My grandpa sent me only one card all my life and I don't remember what it was for, I only remember what he wrote inside: "Climb every mountain, Ford every stream, Follow every rainbow, 'Till you find your dream."

I didn't know this was from *The Sound of Music* at the time, and it doesn't matter now. The essence of what he was trying to tell me is something that has stayed with me all my life, and here we were facing a mountain.

The first four kilometres took us just over an hour. With our breezy attitude knocked out of us, we were shocked by how much we had underestimated the challenge. The next four kilometres took two-and-a-half hours, and at the end of it, Ben, the 16-year-old, threw up with the exertion.

When we finally got somewhere we could stop for the night, there was no help extended; in a salutary way we were made aware that we were 'just another pilgrim' on the road. I had to put Ben to bed half washed and shaking, in communal bunks, and all we had to look forward to was the 6.30am rise for a breakfast of day-old bread and weak tea.

That first day the Pyrenees seemed to slap us in our faces, spin us around, and laugh at our audacity for thinking we could just wander over them. The next day dawned with a gentle mist that cloaked a ferocious heart. It threw everything else at us.

These horses neighing on the mountainside, and being answered by the herd on the crest of the hill, made Harry, the 12-year-old, squeal with delight. The sheep wander freely, looking like woolly rocks, the cowbells clinking with the rhythm of happy grazing. You can hear the crickets and it is all undeniably beautiful. But you can also hear the churning of your blood pounding through your veins.

What that blazing sun and those blue skies don't show is a wind birds couldn't take off into; a punishing, cold wind that whipped the air out of every breath and seared your skin as it blew past.

As we pulled slowly over one brow of undulating terrain, the hills rolled ahead with a seasick relentlessness.

Ben threw up for five hours, he couldn't even keep water down. Frustrated with his brother's constant need to stop and rest, Harry walked away.

I couldn't hold Harry back, I couldn't leave Ben.

Can you imagine what that is like for a mother? I had to dig deep inside and trust that I knew the person Harry was, remind him to stay on the path, and watch him go.

Then there was just Ben and I left on the hillside.

Taking his backpack from him, I watched Ben sit down and cry because he couldn't carry on. Then, he looked across the hillside opposite him to a cross marking a grave, and realised he had no choice.

It is true that you can only do so much for your children. You can take all the weight you like off them but you can't do it for them. All you can do is stand beside them and be there.

We inched our way over the 1,450-metre Col de Lepoeder peak. It was as far to go back into France as it was to push on into Spain. There was nothing around for miles, no off-ramp, no convenience store, nothing.

All I could suggest was that Ben vomited with the wind as washing his walking boots wasn't an option.

Again he sat down, and I watched his eyes roll back in his head as he went clammy and pale. I stood looking at a simple, bleached-wood-and-wire fence running down the slope away from me and wondered what kind of mother doesn't carry glucose tablets. We hadn't spoken English to anyone since we set off. A few minutes later a young man walked up to us and asked if Ben was OK, in a perfect Cambridge accent. He then said: "I don't know if they'll be any help, but I've got a packet of Lucozade tablets if you want them?"

In that moment I understood that this was what every day was going to be like.

It took us two days to walk 24 kilometres.

776 KILOMETRES TO GO

The next two days disappeared down a trail of being weighed and measured at every turn. They were the hottest days on record and it was a maelstrom of sleep deprivation and pre-dawn set-offs, getting lost in the dark, and trying to find a bank as you need cash for everything, sitting in any patch of shade we could find in 33-degree heat wishing for a waterfall, and then finding

one. Walking down tracks with shadows cast like delicate ladders to step along, and down trails that disappeared like rabbit holes with no known end, often passing cenotaphs as evidence of failed attempts to walk this route. Then we came across a man kneeling on the floor weeping, because he had become separated from his friend. An hour later Ben asked me if Harry was all right. He was

ahead of us, again, but had stopped. By the time we got to him he was crying. He had wanted to walk this to bond closer with us and yet he was the one who was walking ahead in frustration, and he understood the consequences of losing us now. I took his backpack and we kept going, together. We arrived at Arras, the first town we had seen for three days.

I was glad to see the end of the trail because I was beginning to lag behind. The blisters I developed coming down off the Pyrenees were really burning.

As we turned into the main street we saw an old man fall against a wall. A young man jumped up to help and the next moment the old man collapsed. A café chair was brought, the local police were on the scene and we had to step out of the way of the Red Cross.

Once we knew he was all right I noticed I had slowed to a shuffle and was bent over too. It took me a moment to really appreciate I wasn't going anywhere. It was one of the hardest things to do to turn to my sons and admit that somewhere over the last 69 kilometres all my invincibility had been beaten out of me. I couldn't walk anymore. All three of us had found our nadir over those three days.

We took a bus into the city of Pamplona; after two days walking through the countryside it had a certain smell; of groomed people and dry-cleaned clothes worn to the soundtrack of heeled shoes in a rush.

The first music we had heard in a week drew us like moths, but the musicians themselves were passed by like so much detritus on the street. Those streets seemed worn down from having to hold up the lifestyle of a city, exhausted by keeping up the performance of serving endless expectations and the anticipation of countless dreams.

We headed out and ended up in a refuge on the outskirts of Pamplona. An utterly ordinary place run by an extraordinary woman, called Maribel, who peered out from under the peak of her baseball cap to assess you as you walked in, with uncanny accuracy. In between telling us that "hot drinkings and cold drinkings and wifee [sic]" were available, she took one look at me and told me weight was my problem - I was carrying too much - and to bring my feet to her at six o'clock.

To have your feet washed and cared for by a stranger is humbling. She syringed my blisters and taped my feet. She taught me how to tie my boots to stop my feet slipping in them on descents, as her father had taught her. Kindness is as beautiful as dew on a spring flower, a drop of life-giving sweetness that makes us believe in our humanity again. When you truly accept it from strangers it opens up an inner light that reflects the world in a different way.

We took a rest day, for me. That day Eve and Hannah, mother and daughter from England, came into our lives. Eve was trying to complete the pilgrimage again having had to leave the first attempt with her eldest daughter through injury. We suddenly understood, through their story, that it was not inevitable that we would reach the end.

In the beginning, when people ask if you are going to Santiago, you say, "Yes."

By day five, the answer is, "I hope.

It was suggested that we put our backpacks in a taxi for two days to help me recover. I had to admit to the boys that the woman who brought them this far was fallible. I was a threat to our chances of doing this and I had to accept the help of the taxi. It became about being able to stay on the road and not about being perfect.

We set out again in a new, wiser dawn that seemed untouched by the complexity of an industrial and technological world. We walked from the wheat fields of the valley floor up to the windmills surfing the horizon, evoking Don Quixote's battle with those in his mind. At the crest of Alto de Perdon (the peak of forgiveness) is a well-known sculpture of silhouettes said to represent the eternal nature of the walk. The whole of the walk is an extended allegory, a complex metaphor, a trope for life... and forgiveness, of course, is something you give to yourself.

We heard a story that night that resonated by coincidence. Traditionally you take a stone from home with you to represent your burdens and you put it down symbolically at the Iron Cross, in preparation for the final phase of the walk. However, our storyteller told us you can put your stone down at any time along the way and someone will pick it up and carry it for you for a while. It is all right to accept help. In turn, you too can pick up someone's stone and carry it for a bit. This way all stones get there eventually.

17

One week and 120 kilometres into the walk feels like nothing and everything. When we finally met up with our backpacks again we rid ourselves of everything we didn't need to carry – and yes, it is a metaphor for shedding the baggage we carry in life.

It was necessary if we wanted to survive the journey, and it was cathartic for tired minds and souls, which were on their own journeys.

I even threw out my sleeping bag; for one hour between three and four in the morning it was very cold, but for 23 hours of every day I did not miss it.

The baggage we carry serves a positive purpose; much like a sleeping bag, we carry it because it protects us in some way. But the longer we live, the difficulty becomes not how far we can go, but the challenge of traveling light.

Funny, I thought we really had only packed the bare essentials. We all downsized, from three backpacks to one between us. This was now too heavy for any one of us to carry across the distances we were traveling so we taxied it until we found a town big enough to buy new ones.

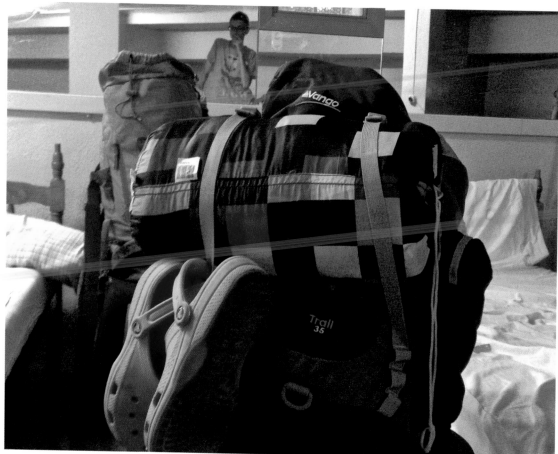

Just to show you the difference, I went from the blue backpack to the silver one at its side - you should only carry ten per cent of your body weight.

Everything I carried from then on fits on an A1 piece of card, including my reliance on a little tech; it was everything I needed to sustain me over 33 days.

You need a change of clothes to wear while you wash the ones you walk in, and something to sleep in. You need one warm top, a swimming costume is useful if only to

wear while washing your clothes sometimes, and a pair of casual shoes to change into gives your feet a rest and lets your boots air at the end of each day.

A wash bag of what you need to keep yourself clean, a small towel, a first aid kit, necessary documentation and anything else you really cannot live without. For me that was my camera.

Imagine if everything we really needed in life fitted on an A1 piece of card.

From that day on, sunflowers lined our route, waving their pompom heads and cheerleading us on. As they always follow the sun, they are thought to symbolise enlightenment, but they remind me of a Maori saying "Face the sun and let the shadows fall behind you."

680 KILOMETRES TO GO

You take yourself on the walk; it is about you and how you handle any challenges. It isn't the difficulty of the road that matters; it's how we react that defines us. It is precisely the ability to keep going when it's tough and uncomfortable that makes the difference. To see the beauty and dare to find the lessons is the secret key of life.

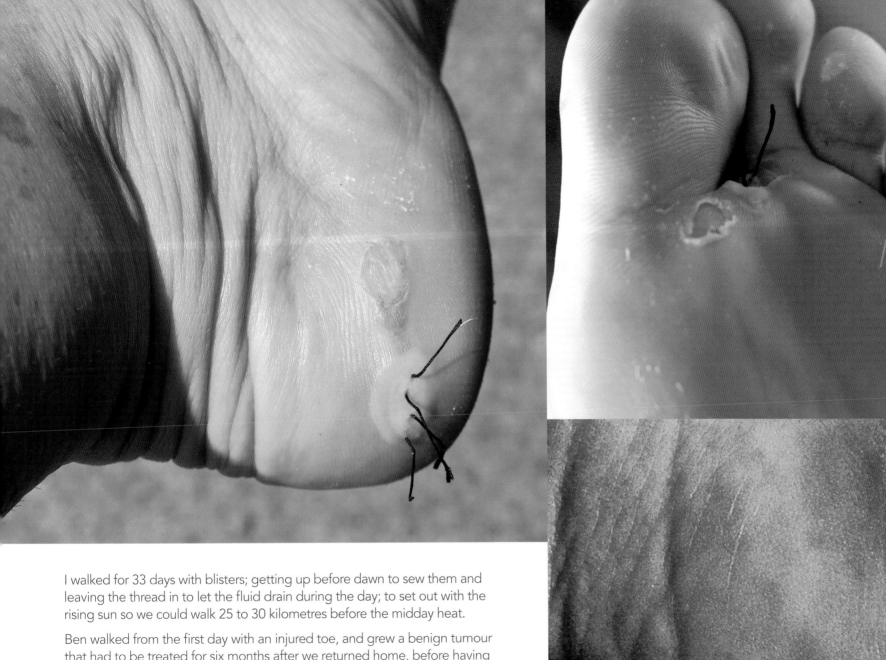

I walked for 33 days with blisters; getting up before dawn to sew them and leaving the thread in to let the fluid drain during the day; to set out with the rising sun so we could walk 25 to 30 kilometres before the midday heat.

Ben walked from the first day with an injured toe, and grew a benign tumour that had to be treated for six months after we returned home, before having the nail surgically removed.

The 12-year-old bounced all the way, but on the other hand Harry had to learn to consider others and walk at my pace.

Every day the walk was long, tiring, challenging, across vast landscapes, some staggeringly beautiful, others harsh and unforgiving. Often the way was through environments that weren't inspiring, like cement factories and industrial outskirts. Remote villages have few amenities and comfort isn't readily available.

In some ways you get stronger but in many ways you get worn down; the food is inadequate, the water can make you sick, and toilet breaks in the middle of nowhere are a challenge.

You have to find somewhere to sleep at the end of each day, in a new place, and negotiate for your accommodation, which can be basic: bunk beds with plastic mattresses and 50 people sharing an outside sink and a shower, which can be short, cold, and communal. There is no certainty you will get a bed, you simply have to move on until you do. Your traveling companions come in all sizes and body shapes, ages, ethnicities, and temperaments. Sleep deprivation comes with the territory.

This life takes courage; sometimes we have no choice, at other times it takes a leap of faith. We need courage to get up every day and get out there. Right at the point of admitting we were uncertain we found we were simply at the edge of our comfort zones.

When we didn't know how we would do something, we just leaned into it and took a step.

Over whatever meagre breakfast we found ourselves offered, we'd have a conversation about what we would like to get from the day, like setting an

intention, and then we made a habit of noticing all the good, and found nothing has quite the same magic touch that gratitude has to make a day feel special.

You don't have to do this, so you have to choose to get up and walk again, every day.

But from the moment you walk out into the unknown every step gives you courage…

and you can spend the day enjoying the best show nature can put on. There are dawns where the landscape sits like an undefined rough idea waiting to be coloured in with more thought later.

You are right in the middle of it all before everything wakes up; deep in that world where there are no memories, between the dark and that moment just before waking into a brand new world. When the sun seeps through the windows in the rooms of your mind and dissolves the night.

Through woods with yellow and white trees to rolling red hills, open golden fields, and patterned skies, nature is applied with the gentlest touch.

From bare, minimalist landscapes to tunnels of light and knotted drama. To vast 360-degree, ocean-blue skies at midday, and deep velvet, luxurious evenings that cool down into glittering night skies. Where a second can expand into an undefined tranquility as if it has forgotten something it never knew, and nothing is rushed.

Then you go from towering trees against pastel skies to gloriously intricate frescos ten metres high, within the most articulate architecture. When you walk into a town often the church is the only thing to see, so you go in. The incredible capacity of the human spirit is celebrated in the stonework, the harmony of design, the imagination and physics, giving meaning to everyday rituals.

The space is not like any secular building...

you know you are not in a gym...

or an office...

or a shopping centre...

When you walk into a space designed by Antoni Gaudí during organ practice, or you hear the sweetest music cascading down from these arches as you are bathed in the light of a rose window, you see that every gravity-defying arch, and rhythmic pattern and embellishment, brings reason and thought and premeditation to the intoxicating everlasting song of veneration.

When you stand among the life-size, extravagant sculptures or shelter in the intimate haven at the heart of a community, or sit facing the grand and sophisticated Baroque reredos at a high alter, or rest in the contemplative space…

You see the very best of our creative and spiritual capabilities, concentrated in one small, but overwhelming, step through a door. This is the best of human nature.

When you have looked into the eye above a 50-kilogramme Botafumeiro swinging 21 metres above you, the redemptive power of art stares right back at you.

We didn't do any of this alone, we had help and friendship along the way.

The company on the road is a mosaic of the world. Complete strangers pop up for a few hours, others become firm friends. Right from the start we met wonderful people like Jacques, a short, leathery, elderly man, who spoke no English and worked in the refuge on our first night. On our first morning he went to find strawberry jam for the boys' stale bread and told them he noticed how they treated their mother. He insisted on kissing my forehead and telling me he thought the boys were special while telling them to stand straight and stay strong.

The Basque activist, Jon, carried Ben's backpack for two hours on that terribly hard second day. He told us all about The Battle of Roncevaux Pass - which the guerrilla army of the Basques won on Saturday 15th of August in the year 778 - before he turned back at the descent into Spain.

Joe is from New York and training to be a doctor; we met in a hostel in Logroño, the city of the Rioja region. We kept bumping into each other, almost without exchanging a word, until we ate at adjoining tables in Atapuerca, an archaeological site of the earliest human beings in Europe. He had walked The Camino before, so we asked if there was somewhere we should not miss, and that is how we came to be in Hontanas, a dot sunk into a plateau with a population of 70.

There he introduced us to Sue. She is a florist and, like Aphrodite, the goddess of love and beauty, she spreads smiles like rose petals down a bridal aisle. This was her fifth walk and she stayed with us for days, guiding us to great food and favourite refuges and becoming part of an extended family.

Ronelle is a South African woman who put enough meals in the freezer for her husband and left him with the dogs to walk this alone. She agreed that we should not attempt a notoriously difficult section of the walk and then told me about some of the unmissable parts, all of which just happened to be in that area. They turned out to be the very best part of the walk for us.

There was the school pastor, Matt, who gave us the glucose tablets; ever-smiling Harini from Vancouver who saw the good in everyone and had a sense of adventure that lifted her face ever onward. Alice and Alosha from Australia, who got engaged on the way; Jade who walked with shattered shins; Paula who was walking for the second time, grateful she was able to after finding a tumour on the first attempt. Susannah, who bought my sons their first sangria; Juan, from Spain, who was looking for love but was really learning to love himself; Michael and Tom from Germany; Who from Korea; Jun from Japan, and so many others.

Eve is the English mother walking for the second time with her youngest daughter, Hannah, who taught us that it isn't a given that you will walk to the end.

The last couple is Richard and Cecelia, who walked from Nuremberg. They had already been walking for over 2,000 kilometres by the time we met them. Richard was 81 and Cecelia was 69 and was walking on chemotherapy after a double mastectomy. Everyone has a story, and every story played a part in ours. Meeting people is always a recognition of a part of you. They all shone a light on a little of our path.

All these people brought something to our journey, and they also accepted our part in theirs. Children were not always welcome; we were turned away from three places and only cautiously welcomed at a few refuges because people assumed children would be disruptive. Many people chose not to walk with us as we didn't fit their story.

There were those we did not get on with. The road carries with it the values of the pilgrimage: gratitude, compassion, optimism, honesty, love, hope, companionship, tolerance, acceptance, openness, and mutual dependency as a community. If you share this outlook, you feel normal. If not, you stand out; and there were those whose attitude veered wildly from these values and it grew arduous to accompany them. You become like the company you keep so it is all right to prefer people whose values you share, and it was easy to do with the wonderful people we met.

You walk into the end of your day and it comes down to what really matters: you need a shower, and a chance to wash your clothes in time for them to dry the next day.

You need the fellowship of good company, something to eat, a little wine, and a bed. That's all that really matters. Then you get up and do it all again.

Church bells are a part of every day. The first time I truly heard them was when we walked into Puente la Reina at midday; a town where all roads finally meet to become one. A stentorian sound of large bronze bells rang from each opening of the tower, which rose straight up like a bold and monumental stone sentinel over the medieval town.

We were subsumed into a vortex of vibration, each full circle of the bells rising and falling in the most magnificent clarion call to life I have ever heard.

Wave after wave reverberated down the narrow streets of grand houses with projecting eaves, decorated with shields, and graceful balconies covered with geraniums. The high narrow walls held the sound like the tines of tuning forks; a solid wall of resonance vibrated through my body obliterating idle thought to become almost meditative. I felt alive in rare ways.

After this I would hear church bells and be drawn to the chance to stop the day and get off for a while, to pause in a silence inside. How wonderful it would be to hold every moment with such wonder, and search it for the stories of the universe. An hour in silence can be a pilgrimage.

462 KILOMETRES TO GO

No four kilometres are like any other four kilometres, and you don't always know where you are going. You have to make decisions in the moment all day, every day, and keep moving even though your muscles ache and your back bows in submission to the endurance. Imagine what weft of extremes a day can weave through.

One morning we got up at 5am to leave Burgos, a grand, robust city that gave birth to the conquering military prowess of a man like El Cid, and The Laws of Burgos, which first governed the Spanish treatment of Native Americans in 1512.

For five perfect minutes we sat on a cold, dewy bench under a street lamp, eating the best ham and cheese pasty we have ever tasted, piping hot, straight from the baker's tray. Then we spent nearly three hours walking to get beyond the grip of the city, around the banks of overpasses, through tunnels of graffiti, under power lines, and along train tracks.

There is no way to understand how hard it is to walk out of a city until you have to do it. The energies of the infrastructure that fuels a city generate a foul gloom. We were in very bad moods, bickering, and struggling in a fetid air that surrounded us like a ground mist. We had to put cloth across our faces to breathe through the smell; because you cannot escape anything quickly when you are walking. I had a headache.

Then suddenly we moved past the adversity of tall towers carrying electricity overhead and the electrified tracks and cables encircling the city boundary, and crossed a low bridge over a shallow stream. A small patch of sunflowers greeted us, the track turned a soft white and our mood lifted. It was as though we had passed beyond an invisible urban dome.

Within 20 minutes this was where we found ourselves. There is no way to tell what it took to get here, and from here you could not see what was around the corner. I was simply here, now. The misshapen memories of injuries of a thousand yesterdays and the lure of any tomorrows were made powerless in the deep breath of the present.

This is where the magic really started to happen.

We were facing six days on the Meseta Central – a plateau in the heart of peninsular Spain. It's a 240-kilometre walk across flat, dry, wheat fields interrupted by the occasional town. No shade, no breeze, just hot, arid and relentless horizons.

People talked about this stage for days before, many skip this part, most of the people we met so far were taking the train round it.

Its tough reputation is legendary, so hard I thought maybe I was being careless taking the boys into it; but this is also what we had been told not to miss. The night before, I was still debating whether we should do it, particularly when we found out there was no public transport out of the area for the next three days.

The boys said they were prepared for it, so we decided we would go…

The air was thick with heat and wheat dust, kicked up by the reaping, threshing, winnowing combine harvester rotors.

There was an endlessness about the horizon and an immediacy about the details at your feet; the walk seemed both relentless and ever-changing at once.

It is a remarkable feeling to face nothing.

The silence is a pressure at first.

But slowly the land and the heat won out against the noise, and we fell into a companionable silence. In that expanse of nothing every pulse of internal driving force was uninterrupted, a place of profound peace that allows you to narrow your life down to that heartbeat.

You begin to recognise habitual patterns of thinking, and this allows you to respond in new ways; in this relaxed state the mind is clear and you connect with a deeper sense of purpose and appreciation of all the small things which give life real meaning.

You walk in the heat for a long time, your mind is taken down the empty road ahead, your thoughts have the silence in which to be heard, and they crowd your head. You can talk to distract yourself, but ultimately you walk alone with only your thoughts.

For hours… and then slowly you can even let your thoughts go silent…

and a lasting peace is found inside.

You can feel your core growing stronger, and that makes you feel like you are carrying less emotional weight. After all the silly games are played and you walk into the end of the day, the dogs stop barking and chasing their tails and lie down, and the evening stretches and reaches down deep inside you to open a space in which you can hear the Earth whisper.

We hauled into a little one-street town nestled at the bottom of a dip and sat at the end of the day with a drink and crisps. Everything felt as if it had woken from a one-hundred-year sleep under a spell, every cell in my body felt conscious, every thought in my mind was engaged, concentrated, moved. Everything was alive and I could feel the pauses between time, and I knew these birds were going to fly before they did.

51

All your senses are so wide awake you can almost taste the colours, you can hear unheeded sounds and see things with an intense clarity. Even a grasshopper three metres away, low down on a bracken leaf swaying in the wind. A bee's wings became silver flashes of laced light and elusive cicadas came out into the open.

No matter how hard the walk there was always something inspiring, even if it was only a rose blushing in the early morning light in the shelter of an ordinary wall. The road is full of beauty, bursting like small fireworks of sublime details that make you live in the unwritten weave of a nature poem. You feel you can believe in dreams.

Each day lowered us deeper into the experience, like a canal lock for life. Two days later we got up as if all this was normal, and everything all day seemed to unfold with a surreal euphoria. I felt like we were a comedy troupe wandering through an *al fresco* medieval play full of ludicrous Chaucerian touches, caught between comedy and control as if the axis of the earth we walked had shifted.

Everyone seemed to be having their happiest day. After breakfast, a man who parked his car across the path and insisted on writing homilies in our Credentials, was giving out sweets and muttering about his great art works. He told us of his sculptures to the spirit of the pilgrimage, his life's work in his orchard. He insisted we take a detour to see them and stood in front of them, pointing out their detail: the hair, the hat, the painted toenails on what turned out to be scarecrows made from tree trunks. Even though not everyone who appears among you and announces a miraculous sign or wonder is a prophet, for an hour he felt like a great artist finally appreciated.

By lunchtime we were eating with Emilio, a donkey who had a taste for cheese sandwiches. He didn't like chorizo though and had mastered the art of banging the sandwiches on the furniture to knock the spicy sausage out; and then he finished off the crumbs scattered on the table. Although not every dinner companion brings something to the table worth having, for an hour everyone enjoyed the absurdity.

Amongst all the ridiculous and fantastical episodes, from the still, quiet pause in a day, rose something truly pure.

This scene of two boys walking off down an ordinary backstreet in the middle of nowhere in particular seems unremarkable, but it holds the story of a life-changing moment.

Six kilometres out from Carrión de los Condes, down a side street in Villalcázar de Sigra, we stopped in a little bar for a much-needed drink. I felt like I had been walking since the 13th century and was grateful for a break. When I stood up to get back on the road again, there was a searing pain in my knee so sharp I sat right back down again.

Next to our table was an advertising board with a taxi number on it. Harry looked at me sideways and said, "Maybe it's a sign."

Amused that he used this to his advantage, I gave in and agreed we'd take a taxi. Both my sons turned to me and said: "No, you're taking a taxi, we're walking."

This was the last time I saw my boys. The next time I saw them, they were men.

Eighteen months ago, on that ordinary Tuesday night in February when the boys stood up as the credits rolled on our TV screen and said they wanted to walk 800 kilometres to Santiago de Compostela, I knew, no matter how hard it was, I had to make it happen.

Watching them walk away, I realised that this was why I had walked all this way.

Nothing quite prepares you for watching your sons grow up in front of your eyes; knowing you will never quite be the same person again.

I could never have imagined I would watch them do it. When I woke up that morning there was no indication that this would be the day. As I bought three bottles of soft drink from the bar, it never crossed my mind that it was going to happen right then.

It's extraordinary how some significant moments are so quiet you would hardly know they were there.

As a parent, we want to conjure a wind underneath our children's wings, not so they can fly but for them to soar high with passion and joy. I have no end of failings as a mother but in walking away they showed me I had done all right, and I understood that this was the reason I had come on this walk. I was truly at my happiest.

When they left me in that bar to set off for a town, they had no more information than the name of a refuge I would try and get us into. The town wasn't an easy one, it was moderately large and our accommodation was off the main street, tucked down a side road. I resisted the temptation to tell everyone to keep a look out for them and decided to let them figure it out... and they did.

That evening we met up again in the simple reception of the convent refuge, with the singing Augustinian nuns, the gorgeous singing nuns from Columbia. Strangely moving and yet absurd. When they sang Amazing Grace, even the strongest cynic would have folded.

After this the guys went to sit outside a bar in the sun and called my sons over to join them. They had their first boys' night out with the best men, from a dozen different backgrounds, men with values and a sense of wonder and fun, who treated my sons as equals.

You don't get your first boys' night out again, so I left them to enjoy the banter and the sangria they were being bought and wandered off to the church, as I had heard it was worth visiting.

It turned out there was a service for the feast day of The Assumption, a significant day in the Catholic calendar celebrating the belief that Mary was taken into heaven without having to live out her natural life, because she was the mother of Christ.

The priest gave a sermon that I could understand every word of for some reason, about the importance of mothers and the grace of the relationship between mother and child.

This sermon on this day was a powerful coincidence.

By the time the softly-spoken, Columbian nun accompanied herself on an acoustic guitar, singing, "Everything Changes Except Love", I was in tears.

When that sweetly-smiling nun went on to give a speech about Hope and started handing out little paper stars the sisters had cut out and coloured in while praying for us, I gave in and cried for at least the next three days. With pride for my sons, gratitude, joy, relief, a feeling of coming home to myself.

This was the dawn the next day, looking back down 17 kilometres of straight road between yesterday and where we were going. There are moments so vast the quiet burns a new colour in the sky, and the dawn smells different.

380 KILOMETRES TO GO

The walk grounds you, then it breaks you down, before it sets you free.

When there is nothing but soft, white, loose dust left, a branch worn smooth
by sand looks dry and dead except for the very obvious, tiny shoot of life.
From the dust at your feet, new life emerges; as if the very dust breathes.

The truth that you do not have to do this is ever-present; you can hang up your shoes anytime, you have to make an effort to stay on the road.

People leave out of boredom, intolerance for the conditions, lack of time, injury. The choice can get taken away. It is not about a physical strength; we met grown men with years of gym hours in their muscles forced to go home, broken. People survive on handfuls of painkillers.

It is a balance between managing yourself physically, emotionally, and spiritually. One morning we sat down to another 5.30am buffet breakfast of tepid tea, dry mini-muffins, and plain biscuits. This was our 26th dawn; 26 days of scrappy food, pushing 25 to 30 kilometres over different terrains, on 26 nights of interrupted sleep.

Despondency can set in easily in the overbearing monotony of the mundane repetitiveness. You can lose any sense of purpose in the routine, and it is so easy to stew in the juice of your own complaints and be reduced to a shamble.

You can be the plaything tossed like a mouse in the paws of a cat, or you can be the adventurer in search of experience.

You need sufficient hardiness to lean into the wretched melancholy and gloom, to wrestle with your emotional flatline, and find the energy to feel for the heartbeat of the day.

This is when you face the hardest challenge every morning.

This last stretch tests your ability to keep going when there is no obvious reward. It is about daring to see the extraordinary in the simple things, and staying in the moment as you navigate the approaching end of the road.

You have to find new ways to notice the joy, to take delight in the simple things, and to be grateful. You have to encourage your mind to see the magnificence when it is obvious and the wonder in a simple line of blue laundry.

That day we had to dig deep to find resources, and I felt we really needed a hot shower and a bed, and good food and sleep. I wanted to take a breath, and pause, not get caught up in the rush to the finish line. Life is both too short and too long to allow yourself to live it half-heartedly.

We ended up in O Cebreiro, the oldest European settlement, nestled 4,242 feet up a mountain just into the province of Galicia. It is hunkered down in the drag of the weather and winds of time, and it was the perfect shelter from the turmoil of the road.

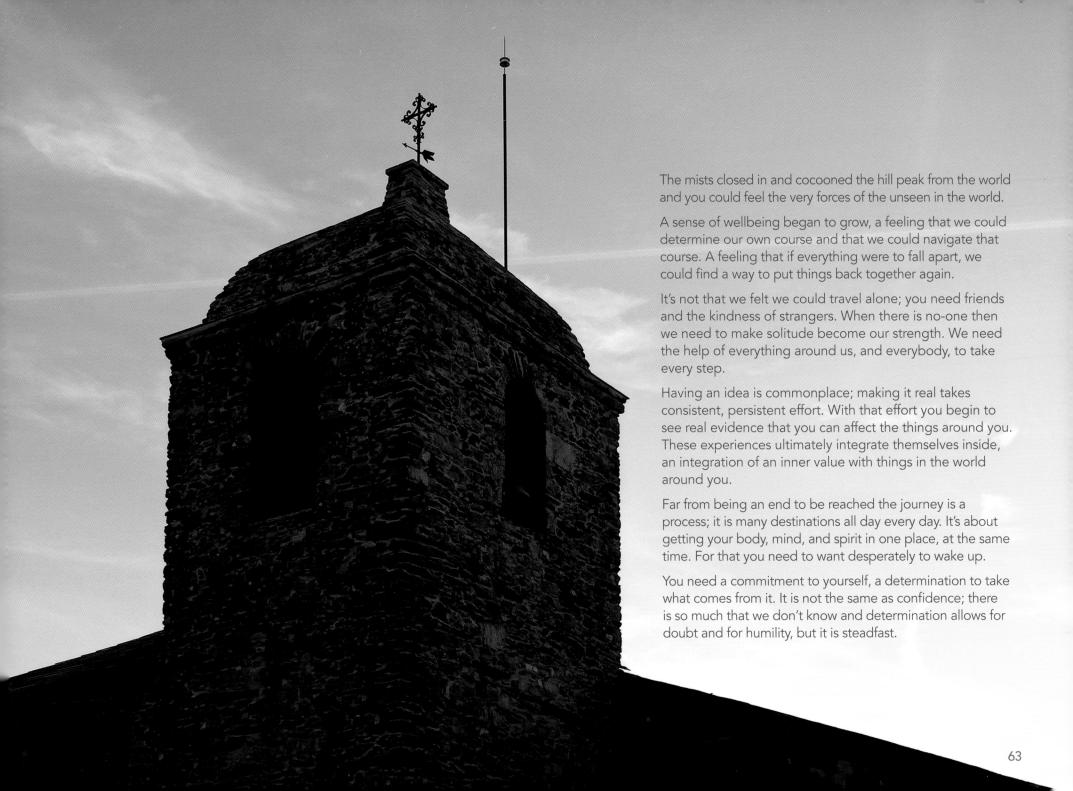

The mists closed in and cocooned the hill peak from the world and you could feel the very forces of the unseen in the world.

A sense of wellbeing began to grow, a feeling that we could determine our own course and that we could navigate that course. A feeling that if everything were to fall apart, we could find a way to put things back together again.

It's not that we felt we could travel alone; you need friends and the kindness of strangers. When there is no-one then we need to make solitude become our strength. We need the help of everything around us, and everybody, to take every step.

Having an idea is commonplace; making it real takes consistent, persistent effort. With that effort you begin to see real evidence that you can affect the things around you. These experiences ultimately integrate themselves inside, an integration of an inner value with things in the world around you.

Far from being an end to be reached the journey is a process; it is many destinations all day every day. It's about getting your body, mind, and spirit in one place, at the same time. For that you need to want desperately to wake up.

You need a commitment to yourself, a determination to take what comes from it. It is not the same as confidence; there is so much that we don't know and determination allows for doubt and for humility, but it is steadfast.

This was the dawn the next day, an unequivocal question in every layer of its beautiful rise asking: "What are you going to do with this one glorious day?"

185 KILOMETRES TO GO

Was it ever fun? All the time. We did the sort of simple things that childish dreams are made of. We lowered the leaves from a tree so that the cows could reach to eat, making them feel like giraffes, if only for a moment. We bought an apple from our food budget to feed to a horse. We met a man walking with a hawk and when it locked eyes with mine, for a split second, I saw everything it had seen and understood what it feels like to fly. We even fed terrapins cat food straight from the tin with a plastic fork.

Of course we met cats and dogs, and saw sheep and pigs, and goats and geese and chickens, but imagine our surprise when we also met an ostrich in the middle of nowhere in particular.

We learnt to enjoy what was there and unleash the silliness that comes out to play for no other reason than because it can. A river of joy meandered through our days, carrying alluvial deposits of fun along with it. Pleasure came from the games we played together as we walked along that brought us closer, happiness came from the ever-changing days in the unconventional adventure. We even found a broken wheelchair in a skateboard park in León and spent an entire afternoon pushing each other around in it. My sons seemed to wear a radiance like a rainbow-coloured superhero cape.

After a while, you realise you are having the best breakfasts of the freshest bread, straight from the baker's hands, with the rising sun. Your first coffee of the day is in the exclusive café off the main street.

your commute is actually a stroll...   with lunch at the best roadside diner...

If you venture to find the special in the ordinary, you can catch a little sun, the spa facilities are incomparable, you get the best seats in the house, have time for meditative contemplation, the night life is jumping, and you sometimes get the penthouse suite. There is always, always something to be grateful for, if you can see with an immortal eye into the inner galaxies of a moment and the confidences of life itself.

There is art everywhere. You only have to look to find it. It is in the cross in the fence that you can make from debris you find on the side of the road. It is in the poster colours that complement the door paint. It is in the silver and gold lines of cut hay. It is in the commissioned art in the square, and where it's accidental, it is in the season's colours and the weathered landscape, and it is right there in your mind.

100 KILOMETRES TO GO

Walking becomes a physical, ritualistic expression of an energetic force. A sense of veneration as a physical act, of gesture, motion, and rhythm. A deliberate movement that begins a surge of sensations on many levels.

Your body feels like a place where life happens; it is a life lived inside you. You can be temporarily, but profoundly, incapacitated yet strangely elated by the exertion at the same time. It is a lassitude state of semi-conscious euphoria. Strong emotions are liberated to play in the field of awareness, and a scarcely-understood imagination can lift you to drift on an expanding sense of inner freedom.

You become aware of your breathing, and can detach from distractions, and wandering images and thoughts, creating a moment to notice the beating of your heart. Your mind naturally focuses attention where time meets eternity.

You discover a clarity of vision and an awareness of unbroken inner light, and a willingness to give yourself over to things you do not fully understand. You can see and feel your connection to everything and that everything is connected. You grow a faith in your ability to honour stillness at some moments and at others to ride the appetite and exuberance of impulse, fully engaged with this strange and shimmering world.

Towards the end the hillsides start to fill out with towns and the road jostles with more people as you gather speed towards re-entry into the real world, and somewhere here you find yourself wandering into towering eucalyptus forests. Just when you need to hold on to the newly-formed solid core inside, you find a depth, significance, and beauty that you may not have noticed before and you can breathe deeply of their heady Antipodean scent, follow their trunks up to the sky, and exhale into the whole universe.

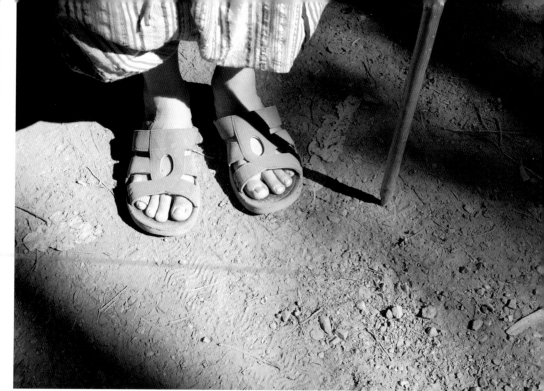

As we walked into Santiago, we were serenaded down a tunnel to the main square and rounded the corner, and we were there.

We were 33 exceptional days and 800 kilometres away from where we began, a lot further than that from our front door, and very far away from that night when we said we would do this. It felt like everything and nothing at the same time.

I thought about my grandpa's message to "climb every mountain..." and thought, "You should see your great-grandsons now, they are amazing."

They became their own people, they gained a certain solid confidence that anybody would appreciate. Harry kept pace with us without thinking about it; he was so relaxed he walked the last four days in a pair of three-euro plastic sandals. He wore a serene smile that was forever playing under the skin at the corner of his mouth.

When we walked into the town of Sarria, two days from the end, we came across a man pushing an elderly gent up a steep hill in a wheelchair, with two women following. He called Ben over and handed the job to him, saying he had to leave and the women couldn't manage. It was all very rapid and surprising, but Ben stepped up to the plate, he didn't hesitate, he didn't look to me for guidance. He just took over pushing the old man up the longest hill right to the top, for an appointment with his doctor. Ben grew up, and literally added five inches to his height.

They are both self-assured and have a solid decency about them. You can see it in them, but how do I know it's true? Because, for the first time in my life, I feel physically and emotionally in one place.

Somewhere in the last 100 kilometres I came across this scene; the sound of every lazy, hot, mid-morning walk in summer drew me to the bees around this tangle of chrysanthemums, and then I noticed the window was opaque and barred. Nobody was looking at the flowers outside the window and yet, unobserved the flowers still bloom.

The thing about a long walk is that you find yourself on a pilgrimage whether you meant to or not.

A pilgrimage is not about rest and recreation at its heart; to set out on one is to throw down a challenge to your life back home.

It cannot help but be a transformational journey because you are tested, inspired, motivated, and humbled every day for as long as you walk. By giving yourself time in which significant change can take place, it is impossible not to discover new insights and find old ones you've forgotten. New places in your heart open up and old, neglected, gossamer-strewn corners are found again.

You find a new understanding and trust in your body. You recalibrate what is most important in your life. Your acuity expands and your sense of spirituality is redefined.

It is a pilgrimage to yourself.

There is one last story.

I met a man; a young and handsome man from Barcelona. It was the day after the singing nuns, and my public display of weeping, and he was amused by me.

He was cool and sophisticated, shaped by the cynicism of the world. Hardened by real life, doubtful of possibility, distrustful of sincerity.

He asked me to explain why I had cried.

Endearingly, when I finished telling him he simply replied that he hoped to have such a moment.

I met him again at the Cruz de Ferro (the Iron Cross), one of The Camino's most emblematic points. It is where you place your stone traditionally and leave all it represents behind. Many leave something meaningful at its base with their deepest wishes. People watch the sun rise, go through the rituals, and turn and hug those they know, hoping their wishes come true for them.

He was supposed to leave at León after five days, but he stayed on the road and I met him again in the church at the top of the highest peak before the descent into Santiago.

We happened to be standing by the confessional box under a small window set in the deep, protective walls, when I asked him if he'd had his moment?

He said, "No. I am dry."

His honesty confronted me. I didn't know how to respond and simply said, "Interesting".

He said, "I don't think it's interesting, I think it's sad."

His yearning created a special place in my heart. We caught sight of each other along the road occasionally, and I saw his face grow softer and his eyes sparkle more each day.

He arrived in Santiago the same morning we did. I came down the stairs of the pilgrim's office and saw him below me in the line for his certificate of completion, the Compostela. I stepped up to him.

It was all there between us in that moment, unsaid.

He burst into tears.

We hugged for the longest time!

For me this very small story describes the big picture… perhaps.

Coming in to Santiago many people throw the shoes they have walked all the way in up to hang off the electric cables overhead as a symbolic gesture of the end.

And of course it is just the beginning.

Because nothing will ever be quite the same again.

MELANIE GOW IS A MOTHER, WRITER, AND PHOTOGRAPHIC ARTIST.

Melanie is from Kitale, a remote town in Kenya, East Africa; her father handed her his Pentax Spotmatic when she was six and her mother taught her to read before she went to school. She has travelled with a pen and a camera ever since.

After studying Art, and Dramatic Art, she went into film-making initially; she was the first British woman director with a film released in cinemas, writing and directing a feature film that was awarded Best Woman Director at the The Festróia Festival Internacional de Cinema de Tróia.

Then she had children and her eldest son became chronically ill. With a change in his treatment he recovered and she spent the next five years researching why her approach worked. Her subsequent book, *Toasters Don't Roast Chickens: the story of an ordinary mum who challenged conventional medical thinking and transformed the health of her chronically-ill child*, was published in 2008.

Writing and Photographic Art have become a way of life. She has travelled with her sons in Australia and parts of Africa, India from north to south, across America from LA to New York. Before walking with them for 33 days over the Pyrenees and across Spain for 800km to Santiago de Compostela.

"To be a mother is the most important post I hold, to take photographs and tell their stories is a privilege."

Michael and Lala Woods
Laura Lucardini
Sian Mah
Kee E-Lene
Kee Shih-Lene
Kee Yong Wee
Daniel Chan Hiok Khiang
Xian Zhen Mah
Pierre L'Allier
Nicole Barty
Kevin Moore
Emma Warness
Connell McMenamin
Lindsey Blake of LibraryLive
John Rendall
Derek Cattani

Yvonne Bilshausen
Annalieze Landa
Tina Harvey
Mel Jones
Anette Snook
Javier Melian
Cecelia Grant-Peters
Alosha Michalenko
Alice Buttenshaw
Caroline Crawford
Robert Brown
Peter Brown
Des Bravington
William Francis Blacklock
Sarah McAllister and
Deborah James of Windsor
Contemporary Art Fair
Harini Nallapothola

Akwa Marina
Valerie McCarthy
Elliot Gibbons
Virginia Bridgman
Edward Marcellus
Daria Marczak
Calum Forsyth
Sue Stephenson
Gail Dorrington
Jackie Couzens
Harriet Burgham
Laurence Olver
Yvonne Bouman
Jeff Alexander
Graham Seaholme
Jacqui Hill
Sally Worman
Suzanne Stallard

Stephanie Butland
Christina Gerritsma
Kathy Rivlin
Donetta Harrison
Ramon Youseph
Simina Astilean
Mehr Keshwani
Tim Wye
Derek Duff
Maggie Brook
Angela Johnson
Tony Gallo
Sally Ann Pollard
Laura Pletti
Fiona Campbell
Sara Jane Asquith
Helena Dennis
Andi Reis
Angela Doyle
Suzanne Samson
Foli Ayivoh
Karen Usher
Ruth Schofield
Hafsa Zubair
Vicci Simpson
Pei Yeou Bradley
Anji Parker
Linda Tyler
Samantha Green
Caroline Bellman Rutter

WITH THANKS

A book is just paper and ink, but from the cover to The End it is a magic carpet that unleashes our imagination, and can transform neurons and lock in new synapses. At no time in history have we had so much opportunity to have a direct and individual influence over what gets published and created, what feeds our less-than-rational sides, our human experience. This book was made possible by those credited here:

Tallulah Rendall
Ben Heron
Caroline Heron
Leigh Glover
Lisa Gee
Josa Young
Martyn Waites
Cheryl Martin
Jo Hatch
Tracy Richards
Yve Audaer
Ruth Humphreys
Clare van Spall
Michael Austell
Rob Lane
David Finch
Helen Williams
Catherine Kidd
Katharine Ross
Juliet Anson
Amanda Bradbury
Jenny Burrows
Wendy McNamee
Danny Grehan
Elizabeth Harvard
Julie-Ann Griffiths
Nick Gilmore
Anita Meszaros
Avril Cartwright
Cathy Boyle Winkler
Julienne Shaw
Tomohiro Iemura

Lisa Ripley
Mark Nolan
Susanna Clark
Chas Newkey-Burden
Essie Fox
Tessa Harris
Sinead Fitzgibbon
Laura Atkinson
Jane Slavin
Vanessa Balkwill
Becky Young
Debs Coady
Carole Williams
Ali Clarke
Helen Cohen
Tara Dominick
Angela Quinn
Claire Dupré La Tour
Bruce and Uta Nelson
Revd. Christopher Evans

Charles Brittain
Olive Elmer Burke
Antony Sharman
Mark Grimes
Mary Feyerherm
Jackie Waller
Jo Schotting
Paola Frigieri
Melissa Jane Dalyanci
Caroline Streatfield-Chalk
Simon Francis Hambrook
Buba Caduzo
Steven Brier
Claire Muttock

What are you going to do with this one glorious day?

Dedicated to my sons, who allowed me walk with them.

"Thank you for being an inspiration."

DEEP ROOTS ARE NOT REACHED BY FROST

from The Riddle of Strider poem, Lord of the Rings, JRR Tolkien

Photographs : Talk : Book

Contact Melanie by email at melgow@me.com

Find out more about her and her work at www.myofficetoday.co.uk